Copyright © 2023 Chimezie Igwe

All rights reserved

The characters and events portrayed in this book are fictitious. Any similarity to real persons, living or dead, is coincidental and not intended by the author.

No part of this book may be reproduced, or stored in a retrieval system, or transmitted in any form or by any means, electronic, mechanical, photocopying, recording, or otherwise, without express written permission of the publisher.

ISBN: 9798867230159
Imprint: Independently published

Cover design by: Art Painter
Library of Congress Control Number: 2018675309
Printed in the United States of America

I0446316

"Success in e-commerce is not just about selling products; it's about creating memorable experiences, building lasting relationships, and embracing the journey of continuous improvement."

CHIMEZIE IGWE

CONTENTS

PREFACE

Welcome to the world of e-commerce, where opportunities abound and innovation knows no bounds. This guide is your companion on an exciting journey through the intricacies of running a successful e-commerce business. Whether you're a seasoned entrepreneur looking to expand your horizons or a newcomer with a dream and a laptop, the principles and strategies shared here are designed to empower you with the knowledge and insights to thrive in the competitive e-commerce landscape.

In a digital age where the lines between brick-and-mortar stores and online marketplaces continue to blur, e-commerce has become more than just a platform for buying and selling. It's a vibrant ecosystem, a dynamic marketplace, and a space where ideas turn into reality.

The world of e-commerce is a dynamic and rapidly evolving one. While this dynamism offers boundless possibilities, it also presents challenges. This guide is your roadmap to navigate this landscape effectively, turning challenges into opportunities and ideas into reality.

We'll explore everything from the inception of your e-commerce venture, including selecting the right products and setting up your online store, to scaling your business, staying compliant with the law, and providing exceptional customer experiences.

You'll delve into the art of branding, the science of marketing, and the critical importance of customer satisfaction.

We'll venture into the world of data protection, intellectual property, and financial management. We'll address the legal aspects, guiding you through the intricacies of licenses, permits, and compliance requirements. You'll discover how to protect your brand and respect your customers' rights while nurturing your own entrepreneurial spirit.

Throughout this guide, we emphasize not only the practical aspects of e-commerce but also the essence of what makes an e-commerce business truly successful. It's about more than just revenue and logistics; it's about making a positive impact, building trust, and leaving a lasting impression.

As you embark on this journey, remember that e-commerce is not just a transaction; it's a relationship. Your customers aren't just numbers on a screen; they're individuals seeking solutions, satisfaction, and trust. Your products aren't just commodities; they're embodiments of your vision, quality, and promise.

This guide is more than just a manual; it's a resource that encapsulates the spirit of entrepreneurship and the ever-changing world of e-commerce. It's here to inspire, educate, and guide you as you embark on your e-commerce adventure.

So, fasten your seatbelt and prepare to explore the exhilarating world of e-commerce. Whether you're a one-person operation or managing a team of experts, the principles and strategies unveiled here are your tools to thrive, your compass in uncharted waters, and your source of inspiration on the path to e-commerce success.

Let's embark on this journey together and chart a course toward your e-commerce dreams.

Chimezie Igwe

INTRODUCTION
The Lucrative World of E-commerce

Welcome to the exciting world of e-commerce, where opportunity meets innovation, and entrepreneurial dreams take flight. In this comprehensive guide, "How to Start a Profitable E-commerce Business: Step-by-Step Guide," we embark on a journey that will equip you with the knowledge, strategies, and insights you need to not only understand the e-commerce landscape but thrive within it.

The digital realm has reshaped the way we conduct business, communicate, and engage with the world around us. E-commerce, short for electronic commerce, is the dynamic force driving the global marketplace into the future. It is a digital symphony of business transactions, consumer choices, and technological marvels. If you're here, it's likely because you've recognized the vast potential that e-commerce holds, and you're ready to dive into this ever-evolving arena.

But, why e-commerce? What makes it such a compelling and lucrative endeavor? Let's begin by exploring some of the fundamental aspects that have made e-commerce an irresistible magnet for entrepreneurs and businesses worldwide.

THE E-COMMERCE REVOLUTION

In the not-so-distant past, traditional brick-and-mortar businesses dominated the commercial landscape. Physical stores, characterized by tangible products and face-to-face interactions, were the norm. Consumers would venture to local shops, malls, and markets to make their purchases. While this model served its purpose, it was not without its limitations.

E-commerce entered the scene as a game-changer, providing a revolutionary shift in how commerce is conducted. The internet's inception brought forth the digital marketplace, where goods and services could be bought and sold from the comfort of one's home, office, or mobile device. The convenience, accessibility, and sheer scale of this transformation have been nothing short of extraordinary.

A WORLD OF OPPORTUNITIES

The digital realm is a vast playground where opportunities are boundless. Whether you're a budding entrepreneur, a seasoned business owner, or an individual with a passion for a particular niche, e-commerce offers a wealth of possibilities.

Imagine having the power to reach a global audience, to tap into niche markets you never thought possible, and operate a business that's open 24/7. E-commerce is not just about selling physical products; it extends to digital downloads, services, subscriptions, and more. The versatility of this platform is only limited by your imagination.

The ability to establish an e-commerce business with relatively low overhead costs has democratized entrepreneurship. You don't need a physical storefront or a massive budget to get started. With the right guidance and strategies, you can navigate the e-commerce landscape with confidence.

THE PATH TO PROFITABILITY

The promise of profitability is a beacon that draws individuals and businesses toward e-commerce. It's no secret that the e-commerce industry boasts immense revenue potential. E-commerce sales have consistently been on the rise, and the potential for growth remains substantial. With a well-conceived plan and the right approach, you can harness this potential and turn your e-commerce venture into a profitable enterprise.

This guide is designed to be your trusted companion on this journey. We'll provide you with a step-by-step roadmap, expert advice, and a wealth of resources to help you understand, establish, and grow a profitable e-commerce business. We'll delve into the intricacies of market research, niche selection, business planning, product sourcing, branding, marketing, customer service, and more. By the time you've completed this guide, you'll be armed with the knowledge and skills needed to navigate the competitive e-commerce landscape successfully.

WHAT TO EXPECT

Throughout this guide, we'll adopt a holistic approach, combining strategic insights with practical, hands-on advice. We understand that you might be a novice looking to dip your toes into the world of e-commerce or an experienced entrepreneur seeking to refine your existing e-commerce business. Regardless of your background, we aim to provide you with rich, educative content that's both informative and actionable.

E-commerce is not just a business model; it's a dynamic ecosystem. It involves a myriad of components that, when well-coordinated, create a profitable and sustainable enterprise. We'll cover these components in detail and ensure you have a comprehensive understanding of each aspect. Our goal is to empower you to make informed decisions, take calculated risks, and ultimately, succeed in the e-commerce industry.

So, whether you're driven by a passion for a specific product, a desire for financial independence, or simply the thrill of entrepreneurship, we invite you to embark on this enlightening journey with us. The world of e-commerce is waiting, and the potential for success is boundless.

Let's begin our exploration of e-commerce, step by step, and uncover the keys to building a profitable e-commerce business. Your journey starts here.

CHAPTER 1
E-commerce Fundamentals

Welcome to the foundation of your e-commerce journey. In this chapter, we will delve deep into the fundamental aspects of e-commerce. By the time we're through, you'll have a solid grasp of what e-commerce is, how it has evolved, and why it's such a compelling field to explore.

1.1 UNDERSTANDING E-COMMERCE: THE BASICS

At its core, e-commerce is about conducting business online. The term "e-commerce" is an abbreviation for electronic commerce, which encompasses all commercial transactions carried out via electronic means. But let's not stop at the definition; let's uncover the essence of e-commerce.

. What is E-commerce?

E-commerce represents a paradigm shift in the way we buy and sell products and services. It's the virtual marketplace where goods and services are exchanged using the internet as the medium. Instead of physical stores, e-commerce relies on digital storefronts where customers can browse, select, and purchase products with a few clicks.

E-commerce is not limited to retail sales alone. It encompasses a broad spectrum of activities, including online banking, electronic ticketing, online auctions, digital downloads, and more. From buying clothes and electronics to booking travel tickets and managing your finances, e-commerce has become an integral part of our lives.

. The Evolution of E-commerce

To truly appreciate the significance of e-commerce, it's

essential to consider its historical evolution. E-commerce didn't emerge overnight but followed a fascinating trajectory.

In the early days of the internet, e-commerce was primarily limited to online catalog shopping. It offered customers the convenience of browsing products and placing orders from the comfort of their homes. Over time, this simple concept evolved into a dynamic ecosystem with increasingly sophisticated features and capabilities.

The introduction of secure online payment methods, robust e-commerce platforms, and innovations in logistics paved the way for the explosive growth of online shopping. Today, e-commerce is not just about selling products; it's about delivering seamless, personalized experiences to customers.

1.2 TYPES OF E-COMMERCE MODELS

E-commerce isn't a one-size-fits-all concept. It comes in various forms, each with its unique characteristics and target audience. Let's explore the most prominent types of e-commerce models.

· B2B (Business-to-Business)

B2B e-commerce involves transactions between two or more businesses. It could be a manufacturer selling components to another manufacturer or a software company providing services to other businesses. B2B e-commerce transactions are typically large-scale, often involving bulk orders and complex negotiations.

· B2C (Business-to-Consumer)

B2C e-commerce is the most common model, involving transactions between a business and individual consumer. When you buy clothing, gadgets, or groceries online, you're engaging in B2C e-commerce. This model is all about catering to the needs and preferences of individual customers.

· C2C (Consumer-to-Consumer)

C2C e-commerce occurs when consumers sell products or services to other consumers. Online marketplaces and auction sites, such as eBay, are classic examples of C2C platforms. Users create listings, set prices, and interact with one another as buyers and sellers.

· D2C (Direct-to-Consumer)

D2C e-commerce has gained prominence with brands choosing to bypass traditional retailers and sell directly to consumers. This approach allows companies to build a more direct and personalized relationship with their customers, often leveraging the power of the internet and social media.

· Omnichannel Retailing

Omnichannel retailing is a blend of different e-commerce models. It involves seamless integration between various sales channels, such as physical stores, websites, mobile apps, and social media. This approach provides customers with a consistent and cohesive shopping experience, regardless of how and where they interact with the brand.

Understanding these e-commerce models is crucial because it will help you determine the right approach for your business. Your choice will depend on factors like the nature of your products, your target audience, and your long-term goals.

1.3 BENEFITS AND CHALLENGES OF E-COMMERCE

E-commerce presents a world of opportunities, but it also comes with its set of advantages and challenges. Let's explore both sides of the e-commerce coin.

- **Advantages of E-commerce**

1. **Global Reach**: E-commerce transcends geographical boundaries. You can sell to customers worldwide, unlocking a vast customer base.

2. **Lower Overheads**: Setting up an e-commerce store is often more cost-effective than establishing a physical storefront. You can save on rent, utilities, and other expenses.

3. **Convenience**: For customers, e-commerce offers unparalleled convenience. They can shop anytime, anywhere, without leaving their homes.

4. **Personalization**: E-commerce platforms can gather data on customer preferences, allowing for personalized recommendations and marketing.

5. **Analytics and Data Insights**: E-commerce businesses can leverage data analytics to gain deep insights into customer behavior and preferences, which can inform decision-making and marketing strategies.

· **Common Challenges**

1. **Competition**: The e-commerce landscape is fiercely competitive. You'll be vying for customers' attention with countless other businesses.

2. **Technical Challenges**: E-commerce requires technological proficiency. You'll need to manage your website, handle online transactions, and maintain cybersecurity.

3. **Logistics and Shipping**: Efficient order fulfillment and reliable shipping are vital. Meeting customer expectations in terms of delivery times and product quality can be challenging.

4. **Customer Trust**: Building trust in the virtual world can be a hurdle. Customers may have concerns about data security and the legitimacy of online businesses.

5. **Constant Adaptation**: E-commerce is ever-evolving. You'll need to stay updated with the latest trends and technologies to remain competitive.

With an understanding of the fundamental aspects of e-commerce and a glimpse of the benefits and challenges, you're ready to embark on your e-commerce journey. In the following chapters, we'll dig deeper into the strategies, techniques, and best practices that will empower you to establish and grow a profitable e-commerce business. Stay with us as we explore the thrilling world of online entrepreneurship.

CHAPTER 2
Market Research and Niche Selection

In the previous chapter, we laid the groundwork for understanding the fundamentals of e-commerce. Now, as we venture further into your e-commerce journey, it's time to explore a pivotal aspect: market research and niche selection. These early steps are akin to a compass that will guide your business toward success. Through careful analysis and informed decision-making, you'll identify opportunities, mitigate risks, and ultimately choose a niche that aligns with your goals and interests.

2.1 THE IMPORTANCE OF MARKET RESEARCH

Market research is the cornerstone of a successful e-commerce venture. It is a systematic process that allows you to gather, interpret, and utilize information to make informed business decisions. Understanding your market is the key to finding a niche that resonates with your target audience and has the potential for profitability.

- ## Market Research Explained

Market research is a multifaceted endeavor that involves various methods and techniques to gather data. It's an essential tool for businesses in all industries, including e-commerce. Here's a breakdown of the key aspects of market research:

- **Consumer Insights**: Gain a deep understanding of your potential customers, their preferences, buying behavior, and pain points.

- **Competitor Analysis**: Analyze your competitors to identify gaps in the market, assess their strengths and weaknesses, and pinpoint areas where you can differentiate your business.

- **Market Trends**: Keep a finger on the pulse of your industry to identify emerging trends and changes in consumer behavior.

- **SWOT Analysis**: Conduct a SWOT (Strengths,

Weaknesses, Opportunities, Threats) analysis to assess your business's internal and external factors.

- **Data Collection**: Utilize a range of research methods, from surveys and interviews to online tools and analytics, to collect relevant data.

- **Tools and Techniques**

Market research involves a toolkit of methods and techniques that can be employed to gather valuable insights. Here are some of the most common tools and techniques:

- **Surveys and Questionnaires**: Collect data from potential customers to understand their preferences and pain points.

- **Interviews**: Engage with your target audience and industry experts through one-on-one interviews to gain deeper insights.

- **Keyword Research**: Use keyword research tools to identify search terms and phrases relevant to your niche.

- **Competitor Analysis Tools**: Explore competitive intelligence tools to assess the strategies and performance of your competitors.

- **Social Media Listening**: Monitor social media platforms for discussions, reviews, and sentiments related to your niche.

- **Google Analytics**: Track website traffic and user behavior to understand your audience better.

- **Market Research Reports**: Access industry-specific reports that provide in-depth data and trends.

Market research may require time and effort, but the

knowledge you gain is invaluable. It will not only guide your niche selection but also inform your business strategies, marketing efforts, and product development.

2.2 FINDING YOUR E-COMMERCE NICHE

Choosing the right niche is one of the most critical decisions you'll make in your e-commerce journey. Your niche defines your target audience, the products you'll offer, and the unique value you bring to the market. To select a niche wisely, consider the following criteria:

- **Niche Selection Criteria**

1. **Passion and Interest**: opt for a niche that genuinely excites you. Your enthusiasm will not only keep you motivated but will also resonate with customers.

2. **Market Demand**: Analyze the demand for products or services in your chosen niche. A healthy balance between demand and competition is ideal.

3. **Competition Analysis**: Assess the level of competition in your chosen niche. Entering a highly competitive market as a newcomer can be challenging.

4. **Profit Potential**: Evaluate the profit margins and revenue potential within the niche. Some niches offer higher profit margins than others.

5. **Target Audience**: Understand your target audience's demographics, interests, and buying behavior. The better you know your customers, the more effectively you can cater to their needs.

6. **Long-Term Viability**: Consider the long-term viability

of the niche. Is it a trend that might fizzle out, or does it have staying power?

7. **Differentiation**: Identify how you can differentiate your business within the niche. What unique value can you offer to customers that others don't?

The perfect niche is a balance between something you're passionate about and something that aligns with market demand. It's where your expertise and enthusiasm meet the needs and preferences of your target audience.

In Conclusion

Market research and niche selection are the initial steps on your e-commerce journey, and they set the stage for your business's future. By investing time in understanding your market and choosing a niche thoughtfully, you position your e-commerce venture for long-term success. In the chapters to come, we'll dive deeper into crafting a solid business plan, selecting the right products, and building a unique brand that will stand out in your chosen niche. Stay tuned, as your e-commerce journey is just beginning, and the possibilities are boundless.

CHAPTER 3
Business Planning and Strategy

In the previous chapters, we laid the foundation by understanding the fundamentals of e-commerce and the significance of market research and niche selection. Now, we move forward into the crucial phase of crafting a well-structured business plan and defining your e-commerce business strategy. These steps are pivotal in ensuring that your e-commerce venture is not just a dream but a reality.

3.1 CREATING A BUSINESS PLAN

A business plan is the roadmap that guides your e-commerce journey. It serves as a comprehensive document outlining your business's objectives, strategies, and the steps you'll take to achieve your goals. Think of it as a strategic blueprint that will shape your e-commerce venture.

· The Components of a Business Plan

A well-structured business plan typically includes the following components:

- **Executive Summary**: A concise overview of your business, including its mission, goals, and the products or services you offer.

- **Business Description**: A more detailed description of your business, its history, the problem it aims to solve, and your target market.

- **Market Analysis**: An in-depth analysis of your market, including your competitors, target audience, and industry trends.

- **Organization and Management**: Information about the structure of your business, key team members, and their roles.

- **Product or Service Line**: A description of your product or service, its features, and how it meets customer needs.

- **Sales and Marketing Strategy**: Your plans for reaching and attracting customers, including your online marketing and advertising strategies.

- **Funding Request**: If you require funding or investment, this section outlines your financial needs and how the capital will be used.

- **Financial Projections**: Projections of your business's financial performance, including revenue, expenses, and profitability.

- **Appendices**: Additional information, such as resumes of key team members, product catalogs, or market research data.

Creating a business plan might seem like a daunting task, but it's an essential exercise that will provide you with a clear direction for your e-commerce business. It's also a valuable document to share with potential investors, partners, or lenders to secure funding.

3.2 E-COMMERCE BUSINESS MODELS

E-commerce offers various business models, each with its unique characteristics. Choosing the right model is a critical decision that will impact your operations, customer interactions, and revenue. Let's explore some common e-commerce business models:

- **Dropshipping**

Dropshipping is a business model where you don't hold inventory. Instead, you work with suppliers who ship products directly to customers. This model reduces your upfront costs, but it requires effective supplier management and a focus on marketing and customer service.

- **Private Labeling**

Private labeling involves selling generic products under your brand's label. You work with manufacturers to create products tailored to your specifications. This model allows you to build a brand and differentiate your products in the market.

- **Wholesale**

Wholesale e-commerce involves buying products in bulk from manufacturers or wholesalers and selling them at a markup. This model requires a significant initial investment in inventory but offers more control over pricing and profit margins.

Each e-commerce business model has its own set of advantages and challenges. Your choice will depend on factors like your budget, business goals, and the niche you've selected. It's essential to thoroughly research and understand the model that best aligns with your vision.

3.3 CRAFTING A UNIQUE SELLING PROPOSITION (USP)

In the highly competitive e-commerce landscape, having a Unique Selling Proposition (USP) is essential. Your USP is what sets your business apart from competitors and compels customers to choose you. Crafting a compelling USP involves the following steps:

- **Differentiating Your Business**

Identify what makes your e-commerce business unique. Is it the quality of your products, exceptional customer service, faster shipping, or a unique product selection? Pinpoint your strengths and what you can offer that others can't.

- **Developing Your USP**

Your USP should be concise and communicate the value you provide to customers. It should answer the question: "Why should customers choose your business over others?" Whether it's a guarantee of satisfaction, an innovative product feature, or a commitment to sustainability, your USP should resonate with your target audience.

Your USP is not a static element of your business. It should evolve and adapt to changes in the market and your customers' needs. Regularly revisit and refine your USP to ensure it remains relevant and compelling.

In Conclusion

In this chapter, we've explored the critical steps of creating a business plan, understanding e-commerce business models, and crafting a Unique Selling Proposition (USP) for your e-commerce business. These elements form the strategic foundation of your venture, setting the stage for your e-commerce journey's success.

With a well-structured business plan, a clear understanding of your chosen business model, and a compelling USP, you're ready to move forward confidently. In the upcoming chapters, we'll explore the practical aspects of setting up your e-commerce store, selecting and sourcing products, building a strong brand, and developing effective marketing strategies. Stay with us as we navigate the path to e-commerce success.

CHAPTER 4
Setting Up Your E-commerce Store

In the previous chapters, we discussed the foundational aspects of e-commerce, including market research, niche selection, and business planning. Now, it's time to dive into the practical elements of setting up your e-commerce store. Your online store is the digital equivalent of a physical retail space, and it's where your customers will interact with your products and make purchases. Let's explore the essential steps to establish a successful e-commerce store.

4.1 CHOOSING AN E-COMMERCE PLATFORM

Selecting the right e-commerce platform is a pivotal decision as it will serve as the backbone of your online store. Your choice should align with your business needs, budget, and technical expertise. Here are some popular e-commerce platforms to consider:

- **Shopify**: Known for its user-friendly interface and extensive app store, Shopify is a great choice for beginners. It offers a wide range of templates and integrates well with various payment gateways.

- **WooCommerce**: This WordPress plugin is highly customizable and offers full control over your e-commerce site. It's a good option if you're already familiar with WordPress.

- **BigCommerce**: BigCommerce is a robust and scalable platform that is suitable for growing businesses. It provides advanced features and customization options.

- **Magento**: Ideal for large and complex e-commerce operations, Magento is an open-source platform that offers extensive customization and scalability. However, it can be complex for beginners.

- **Wix**: Wix offers an intuitive website builder with e-commerce functionality. It's user-friendly and suitable for small to medium-sized businesses.

When choosing a platform, consider factors such as ease of use, scalability, customization, and the costs involved. Many e-commerce platforms offer free trials, so take advantage of these to assess which one best fits your needs.

4.2 DOMAIN REGISTRATION AND HOSTING

Your e-commerce store needs a domain name (e.g., www.yourstore.com) and a hosting service. The domain name should be memorable, reflect your brand, and be easy to type. When selecting a hosting provider, look for one that offers reliable uptime, good security features, and scalability as your business grows.

- **Domain Registration**: You can register a domain name through domain registrars like GoDaddy, Namecheap, or through your chosen e-commerce platform.

- **Hosting**: Your hosting provider can be separate from your e-commerce platform or included as part of the service. Popular hosting providers include Bluehost, SiteGround, and HostGator.

Ensure that your domain name aligns with your brand, and that your hosting provider can handle the traffic and performance requirements of your e-commerce store.

4.3 DESIGNING YOUR STORE

Your store's design plays a significant role in creating a positive user experience and establishing your brand identity. The design should be visually appealing, user-friendly, and reflect the essence of your business. Here are key design elements to consider:

- **Themes and Customization**: Most e-commerce platforms offer a range of themes or templates that you can customize to match your brand's colors, fonts, and style.

- **User-Friendly Design Principles**: Ensure that your store's design is intuitive and easy to navigate. Product categories should be well-organized, and the checkout process should be streamlined.

- **Mobile Responsiveness**: With an increasing number of customers shopping on mobile devices, your store must be responsive and mobile-friendly.

- **High-Quality Imagery**: Use high-quality product images and consider using multiple images to showcase products from different angles.

- **Loading Speed**: Optimize your website for fast loading times. Slow websites can lead to higher bounce rates and lower search engine rankings.

- **Security**: Prioritize website security by using

SSL certificates to protect customer data during transactions.

Your store's design is a vital part of your branding and user experience. It's worth investing time and effort to ensure that it resonates with your target audience.

In Conclusion

In this chapter, we've explored the practical steps of setting up your e-commerce store. Choosing the right e-commerce platform, registering a domain, selecting hosting, and designing your store are essential elements that lay the groundwork for your online business.

With your store taking shape, the next chapters will delve into product sourcing and inventory management, branding, marketing, and customer service. These aspects will bring life to your e-commerce store, making it a vibrant and successful online business. Stay with us as we continue to build your e-commerce venture step by step.

CHAPTER 5
Product Sourcing and Inventory Management

Your e-commerce store is taking shape, and it's time to focus on the lifeblood of your business: your products. In this chapter, we'll explore the critical aspects of sourcing products and managing your inventory. Effective product sourcing and inventory management are key to running a successful e-commerce business.

5.1 SOURCING PRODUCTS

Product sourcing involves finding the right products to sell in your e-commerce store. Your choice of products will influence your brand, customer base, and overall business strategy. Here are some strategies and considerations for product sourcing:

- **Supplier Research**: Identify reliable suppliers or manufacturers for the products you intend to sell. Research their reputation, quality standards, and shipping policies.

- **Negotiating with Suppliers**: Negotiate pricing, minimum order quantities, and payment terms with your suppliers. Build a good relationship with your suppliers for long-term cooperation.

- **Product Selection Criteria**: Choose products that align with your niche, target audience, and brand. Consider factors like product quality, demand, and profit margins.

- **Testing New Products**: Don't hesitate to test new products in your store. Monitor customer response and sales data to determine which products resonate best with your audience.

- **Diversification**: Consider diversifying your product selection to reduce risk. Relying on a single product or category can leave your business vulnerable to market fluctuations.

- **Quality Control**: Ensure that the products you sell meet quality standards. Consistently deliver products that meet or exceed customer expectations.

Successful product sourcing is a blend of research, supplier relationships, and a deep understanding of your target audience. The products you choose will be the building blocks of your e-commerce business.

5.2 INVENTORY MANAGEMENT

Effective inventory management is crucial for your e-commerce store's operations. It involves overseeing the purchase, storage, and tracking of your products. Here are important considerations for inventory management:

- **Stock Control**: Maintain an optimal level of inventory to prevent overstocking or running out of popular products. Utilize inventory management software to track stock levels.

- **Fulfillment Options**: Decide on your order fulfillment method, which could involve in-house fulfillment, dropshipping, or third-party logistics (3PL) services. Each method has its pros and cons.

- **Shipping and Logistics**: Establish efficient shipping and logistics procedures to ensure timely and cost-effective delivery to customers.

- **Returns and Exchanges**: Develop clear policies and procedures for handling returns and exchanges. A hassle-free return process can enhance customer satisfaction.

- **Technology and Software**: Utilize inventory management software and tools to streamline inventory tracking and ordering processes. These tools can automate inventory tasks and provide real-time data.

- **Cycle Counting**: Implement regular cycle counting to maintain accurate inventory levels and minimize discrepancies.

Effective inventory management is essential to prevent stockouts, reduce carrying costs, and ensure that you have the right products available when customers place orders.

In Conclusion

In this chapter, we've delved into the critical aspects of product sourcing and inventory management. Finding the right products, managing your inventory effectively, and delivering quality products to your customers are fundamental to the success of your e-commerce business.

As your e-commerce venture evolves, we'll continue to explore other essential topics such as branding, marketing, customer service, and scaling your business. Stay with us as we build a strong and sustainable e-commerce business step by step.

CHAPTER 6
Building a Strong Brand

Your e-commerce journey continues, and now it's time to focus on a crucial element of your business: branding. Building a strong brand is not just about creating a memorable logo and a catchy slogan. It's about crafting an identity that resonates with your target audience and sets you apart from the competition. In this chapter, we'll explore the multifaceted world of branding and how it can be a powerful asset for your e-commerce business.

6.1 BRANDING BASICS

Let's begin by understanding the fundamentals of branding and why it's so vital for your e-commerce venture.

- **Importance of Branding**:
  - **Trust and Credibility**: A well-established brand conveys trust and credibility to customers. They're more likely to purchase from a brand they recognize and trust.
  - **Differentiation**: In a crowded e-commerce landscape, your brand distinguishes you from competitors. It tells the story of who you are, what you stand for, and why customers should choose you.
  - **Emotional Connection**: Successful brands create emotional connections with their customers. These connections foster loyalty and repeat business.
  - **Perceived Value**: A strong brand can command higher prices. Customers are often willing to pay more for a product from a brand they perceive as high-quality.

- **Brand Elements**:
  - **Brand Name**: Your brand's name is the cornerstone of your identity. It should be easy to remember, unique, and reflective of your niche and values.
  - **Logo**: A well-designed logo is a visual representation of your brand. It should be easily recognizable and scalable for various

applications.

- **Color Palette**: Colors have psychological associations. Choose a color palette that aligns with your brand's personality and values.

- **Typography**: The fonts you use in your branding should be consistent and reflect your brand's character.

- **Slogan or Tagline**: A catchy slogan or tagline can succinctly convey your brand's message and values.

6.2 MARKETING YOUR BRAND

Once you've established your brand, it's essential to market it effectively. Brand marketing goes beyond merely advertising your products; it's about conveying your brand's essence and value to your target audience.

- **Branding Strategies:**
  - **Content Marketing**: Create high-quality, informative content that showcases your expertise in your niche. This can include blog posts, videos, and social media content.
  - **Social Media Marketing**: Utilize social media platforms to engage with your audience and share your brand's personality. Consistency in your social media branding is key.
  - **Email Marketing**: Email campaigns can help you stay in touch with your customers and nurture those relationships. Personalized and relevant content is the key to successful email marketing.
  - **Influencer Partnerships**: Collaborate with influencers in your niche who align with your brand values. Influencer marketing can extend your reach and credibility.
  - **Community Building**: Create an online community or forum related to your niche. Encourage discussions and engagement to foster a sense of belonging.

6.3 BRAND PROMOTION

Promoting your brand requires a strategic approach. Here are some promotional techniques to consider:

- **Content Promotion**: Share your valuable content on various platforms and forums to reach a broader audience.

- **Paid Advertising**: Utilize paid advertising channels such as Google Ads or Facebook Ads to target potential customers.

- **Partnerships**: Collaborate with complementary businesses for cross-promotions or affiliate marketing.

- **SEO (Search Engine Optimization)**: Optimize your website and content for search engines to improve your online visibility.

- **Email Campaigns**: Use email marketing to keep your audience informed about your brand and products.

6.4 BRAND CONSISTENCY

Maintaining brand consistency is vital. Ensure that your brand's messaging, visual elements, and values are consistent across all customer touchpoints, from your website to social media and packaging. Consistency builds trust and reinforces your brand in the minds of your customers.

6.5 BRAND EVOLUTION

As your e-commerce business grows, your brand may evolve. Be open to adjusting your brand strategy to reflect changes in your niche, customer preferences, and market trends. The ability to adapt and evolve is a key aspect of successful brand management.

In Conclusion

In this chapter, we've explored the world of branding, understanding its importance, elements, marketing strategies, and promotion techniques. Building a strong brand is an ongoing process that will set the stage for lasting success in your e-commerce business.

As we continue our e-commerce journey, we'll delve into marketing strategies, customer engagement, scaling your business, and more. Stay with us as we navigate the path to e-commerce success, one step at a time.

CHAPTER 7
Marketing Your E-commerce Business

Now that you've laid the foundation with a strong brand and your e-commerce store is up and running, it's time to focus on reaching your target audience and driving sales. Marketing is the lifeblood of any e-commerce business, and in this chapter, we'll explore various marketing strategies and techniques to help you grow your online presence and attract customers.

7.1 DIGITAL MARKETING STRATEGIES

Digital marketing encompasses a wide range of strategies and channels to promote your e-commerce business. Here are some key digital marketing strategies to consider:

- **Search Engine Optimization (SEO)**: Optimize your website for search engines to improve your organic (non-paid) search rankings. Effective SEO helps potential customers find your products through search engines like Google.

- **Pay-Per-Click Advertising (PPC)**: Launch paid advertising campaigns on platforms like Google Ads or social media sites. You pay for each click on your ad, which can help drive targeted traffic to your site.

- **Content Marketing**: Create high-quality, informative content that provides value to your target audience. This can include blog posts, videos, and social media content.

- **Email Marketing**: Build and maintain an email list to reach out to your customers with promotions, product updates, and valuable content.

- **Social Media Marketing**: Utilize social media platforms to engage with your audience and promote your products. Platforms like Facebook, Instagram, and

Pinterest can be particularly effective for e-commerce.

- **Affiliate Marketing**: Partner with affiliates who promote your products on their websites or through other channels. You pay them a commission for each sale they generate.

7.2 CONTENT MARKETING AND BLOGGING

Creating informative and engaging content is a valuable way to attract and engage customers. A blog on your e-commerce website can serve as a platform to provide in-depth information about your products, industry trends, and more. High-quality content not only drives organic traffic but also positions you as an authority in your niche.

- **Benefits of Blogging**:
  - **SEO Benefits**: Regularly publishing content helps improve your website's SEO, making it more visible in search engine results.

  - **Audience Engagement**: Blogging gives your audience a reason to return to your site, engage with your brand, and build trust.

  - **Education and Value**: Share valuable information, how-to guides, and tips related to your products or industry.

  - **Showcasing Products**: Use your blog to highlight product features, benefits, and use cases.

7.3 SOCIAL MEDIA MARKETING

Social media platforms offer a valuable way to connect with your audience, showcase your products, and drive traffic to your e-commerce site. Here are some tips for effective social media marketing:

- **Platform Selection**: Choose the social media platforms that align with your target audience. Different platforms attract different demographics.

- **Content Strategy**: Plan and create content that resonates with your audience, whether it's through images, videos, or blog posts.

- **Consistency**: Maintain a regular posting schedule to keep your audience engaged. Consistency is key to building a following.

- **Engagement**: Interact with your audience by responding to comments, messages, and participating in conversations related to your niche.

- **Paid Advertising**: Consider running paid social media advertising campaigns to reach a wider audience.

7.4 EMAIL MARKETING

Email marketing is a powerful tool for building and nurturing customer relationships. Here's how to leverage it effectively:

- **Build an Email List**: Encourage website visitors to subscribe to your email list by offering incentives like discounts or access to exclusive content.

- **Segmentation**: Divide your email list into segments based on demographics, purchase history, or engagement levels. This allows you to send highly targeted and relevant messages.

- **Personalization**: Personalize your email campaigns by using the recipient's name and sending tailored product recommendations.

- **Automation**: Use email marketing software to automate drip campaigns, welcome sequences, and follow-up emails.

7.5 PAID ADVERTISING

Paid advertising, such as Google Ads and Facebook Ads, can be a quick way to drive traffic and generate sales. Here are some tips for effective paid advertising:

- **Keyword Research**: Identify relevant keywords for your products and create ad campaigns around them.

- **A/B Testing**: Continuously test different ad variations to determine which ones perform best.

- **Conversion Tracking**: Set up conversion tracking to measure the effectiveness of your campaigns and optimize for better results.

- **Budget Control**: Set a clear budget for your paid advertising campaigns to avoid overspending.

7.6 ANALYTICS AND DATA ANALYSIS

Effective marketing requires ongoing analysis and adjustment based on data and analytics. Use tools like Google Analytics to track website traffic, user behavior, and conversions. Analyze this data to make informed decisions about your marketing strategies.

7.7 CUSTOMER FEEDBACK AND REVIEWS

Encourage customers to leave reviews and feedback on your products and service. Positive reviews can build trust and credibility, while negative feedback can provide valuable insights for improvement. Respond to customer reviews and engage with your audience to build relationships.

7.8 INFLUENCER MARKETING

Collaborate with influencers in your niche to promote your products. Influencers can help you reach a wider audience and provide authentic endorsements for your brand.

In Conclusion

Marketing is an ongoing process that requires planning, experimentation, and adaptation. By implementing effective digital marketing strategies, content marketing, social media marketing, and email marketing, you can attract and retain customers, ultimately growing your e-commerce business. Stay with us as we continue our e-commerce journey, exploring customer service, scaling your business, and more.

CHAPTER 8
Customer Service and Satisfaction

Your e-commerce business is flourishing, and customers are pouring in. In this chapter, we'll explore the world of customer service and satisfaction. Providing exceptional service and ensuring that your customers are delighted with their shopping experience is fundamental to the success and sustainability of your e-commerce venture.

8.1 THE IMPORTANCE OF CUSTOMER SERVICE

Customer service is the backbone of any successful e-commerce business. It's not just about addressing customer issues but also about creating a positive, seamless, and memorable shopping experience. Here's why it's crucial:

- **Customer Retention**: Satisfied customers are more likely to return for future purchases, leading to long-term business success.

- **Word of Mouth**: Happy customers share their experiences with friends and family, serving as free brand ambassadors.

- **Online Reviews**: Positive reviews and feedback can boost your reputation and credibility, attracting more customers.

- **Competitive Advantage**: Excellent customer service sets you apart from competitors and builds trust.

8.2 BUILDING A CUSTOMER-CENTRIC CULTURE

Creating a customer-centric culture within your business is essential. It's about ensuring that every member of your team understands the importance of the customer and is committed to delivering top-notch service.

- **Training and Education**: Train your employees on customer service best practices and ensure they know how to handle different situations.

- **Empowerment**: Empower your team to make decisions and resolve issues promptly. This helps in providing quick solutions to customer problems.

- **Listening and Feedback**: Actively listen to customer feedback and use it to improve your products and services.

- **Customer-Focused Policies**: Develop policies that prioritize customer needs and convenience.

8.3 EFFECTIVE CUSTOMER SERVICE STRATEGIES

To deliver outstanding customer service, consider implementing these strategies:

- **Responsive Communication**: Respond promptly to customer inquiries, whether through email, live chat, or phone. Set clear expectations for response times.

- **Personalization**: Address customers by their names, personalize emails, and remember their preferences.

- **Problem Solving**: Be proactive in identifying and solving customer issues. A smooth returns and refunds process is vital.

- **Transparency**: Be transparent about product availability, shipping times, and pricing. Avoid hidden fees.

- **Quality Assurance**: Ensure the quality of your products or services meets or exceeds customer expectations.

- **Live Chat and Support**: Offer live chat support on your website for real-time assistance. If feasible, provide a customer support hotline.

- **User-Friendly Returns**: Create an easy and hassle-free returns process. Customers appreciate the ability to return products that don't meet their expectations.

8.4 HANDLING CUSTOMER COMPLAINTS

No matter how excellent your service is, you'll occasionally encounter customer complaints. The key is to handle them professionally and turn negative experiences into positive ones.

- **Listen Actively**: Allow customers to express their concerns fully and actively listen to understand their perspective.

- **Empathize**: Show empathy and understanding. Customers want to feel heard and valued.

- **Apologize and Resolve**: If the issue is your fault, apologize sincerely and work to find a satisfactory resolution.

- **Learn and Improve**: Use complaints as opportunities for improvement. Identify trends and patterns in complaints to prevent similar issues in the future.

8.5 MEASURING CUSTOMER SATISFACTION

To assess and improve your customer service, you need to measure customer satisfaction. Here are some methods:

- **Surveys**: Send post-purchase surveys to gather feedback on the shopping experience.

- **Net Promoter Score (NPS)**: Calculate your NPS by asking customers how likely they are to recommend your store to others.

- **Online Reviews and Ratings**: Monitor online reviews and ratings on platforms like Trustpilot, Yelp, or Google Reviews.

- **Customer Feedback**: Encourage customers to leave feedback on your website or through emails.

8.6 LOYALTY PROGRAMS AND REWARDS

Loyalty programs and rewards can help enhance customer satisfaction and retention. Offer incentives for repeat purchases, referrals, or social media engagement.

- **Points-Based Programs**: Reward customers with points for each purchase, which can be redeemed for discounts or free products.

- **Exclusive Offers**: Provide exclusive offers or early access to new products to loyal customers.

- **Referral Programs**: Encourage customers to refer friends and family with incentives like discounts.

8.7 SCALING CUSTOMER SERVICE

As your e-commerce business grows, it's essential to scale your customer service operations to meet increasing demands. This may involve hiring additional support staff, implementing chatbots, or outsourcing customer service.

In Conclusion

Customer service and satisfaction are the cornerstones of a thriving e-commerce business. Providing exceptional service, addressing customer needs, and continuously improving your practices are essential to building a loyal customer base and ensuring the long-term success of your venture.

As we continue our journey, we'll explore topics like scaling your business, international expansion, and legal considerations. Stay with us as we navigate the path to e-commerce success, one step at a time.

CHAPTER 9
Scaling Your E-commerce Business

Your e-commerce business has taken off, and it's time to explore the strategies and considerations for scaling your operations. Scaling means growing your business to accommodate increased demand and, in some cases, expanding into new markets. In this chapter, we'll delve into the essential steps for scaling your e-commerce business effectively.

9.1 THE IMPORTANCE OF SCALING

Scaling your e-commerce business is a critical step that can lead to increased revenue, expanded market reach, and improved profitability. Here are some reasons why scaling is essential:

- **Meeting Demand**: As your business grows, you need to ensure you can meet customer demand and prevent stockouts.

- **Cost Efficiency**: Scaling can lead to cost efficiencies as you benefit from economies of scale in sourcing and production.

- **Market Expansion**: Scaling may involve entering new markets, both domestically and internationally, to reach a broader customer base.

- **Competitive Advantage**: Expanding your product range and services can give you a competitive edge in the market.

9.2 EFFECTIVE SCALING STRATEGIES

Scaling requires careful planning and execution. Here are some strategies to consider:

- **1. Expand Product Lines**: Introduce new products or product categories to diversify your offerings and appeal to a broader audience.

- **2. Improve Logistics and Supply Chain**: Streamline your supply chain, reduce lead times, and optimize shipping and fulfillment processes.

- **3. Invest in Marketing**: Increase your marketing efforts to reach a larger audience, both through digital marketing and traditional advertising.

- **4. International Expansion**: Consider expanding to international markets to tap into new customer segments. Research local customs, regulations, and preferences before entering new markets.

- **5. Optimize Your Website**: Ensure your website can handle increased traffic and is user-friendly. Enhance the user experience and mobile responsiveness.

- **6. Customer Retention**: While acquiring new customers is essential, don't overlook customer retention. Loyal customers provide a steady source of revenue.

- **7. Partnership and Collaboration**: Collaborate with complementary businesses or influencers to reach new audiences and gain credibility.

9.3 FINANCIAL CONSIDERATIONS

Scaling requires an investment of time and money. Here are some financial considerations to keep in mind:

- **Budgeting**: Create a detailed budget for your scaling efforts. Include costs for marketing, inventory expansion, staff, and technology.

- **Financing**: Explore financing options, such as business loans or investors, to secure the necessary capital for scaling.

- **Revenue Projections**: Develop realistic revenue projections to understand the returns you can expect from scaling.

9.4 TECHNOLOGY AND AUTOMATION

Leverage technology and automation tools to streamline your operations. This includes using e-commerce platforms that can handle the demands of a growing business, inventory management software, and customer relationship management (CRM) tools.

- **Inventory Management**: Implement an advanced inventory management system to track and optimize inventory levels.

- **Analytics**: Use data analytics to gain insights into customer behavior, market trends, and the performance of marketing campaigns.

- **Customer Service Automation**: Employ chatbots and AI-powered customer service tools to handle routine inquiries, freeing up your team to focus on complex issues.

9.5 SCALABILITY ASSESSMENT

Before scaling, conduct a scalability assessment to ensure your business can handle the growth. This includes evaluating your existing infrastructure, personnel, technology, and suppliers.

- **Team and Staffing**: Assess whether you need to hire additional staff, including warehouse workers, customer service representatives, and marketing professionals.

- **Infrastructure**: Ensure your website and hosting can handle increased traffic without downtime or slowdowns.

- **Supplier Relationships**: Confirm that your suppliers can meet increased orders and delivery demands.

9.6 RISK MANAGEMENT

Scaling involves risks, including overextension, financial instability, and market changes. Develop a risk management plan that identifies potential challenges and outlines strategies for mitigating them.

9.7 CUSTOMER SERVICE AND QUALITY CONTROL

As you scale, maintain a strong focus on customer service and product quality. Consistently deliver excellent service to keep customers coming back and referring others.

In Conclusion

Scaling your e-commerce business is an exciting and challenging endeavor. By implementing effective strategies, managing your finances wisely, leveraging technology, and maintaining a strong focus on quality and customer service, you can successfully expand your business and secure its long-term success.

In the next chapters, we'll delve into international expansion, legal considerations, and other key aspects of running a thriving e-commerce business. Stay with us as we continue to explore the path to e-commerce success.

CHAPTER 10
Legal and Compliance Matters

Running an e-commerce business involves adhering to various legal and compliance requirements. Ensuring that your business operates within the bounds of the law is essential for long-term success and avoiding potential legal issues. In this chapter, we'll delve into the key legal and compliance considerations for your e-commerce business.

10.1 BUSINESS STRUCTURE AND REGISTRATION

Before launching your e-commerce business, you need to establish a legal structure and register your business. The specific requirements may vary depending on your location and the type of business structure you choose. Here are some common options:

- **Sole Proprietorship**: In this structure, you and your business are considered one legal entity. You have full control and responsibility for your business but also assume all the liabilities.

- **Limited Liability Company (LLC)**: An LLC offers a level of personal liability protection. Your personal assets are separate from your business assets. The requirements and benefits of forming an LLC vary by jurisdiction.

- **Corporation**: Corporations provide strong liability protection, but they involve more extensive administrative requirements and formalities. You may choose to establish an S corporation or C corporation, each with its own tax implications.

- **Partnership**: If you have a business partner, you may opt for a general partnership, limited partnership, or limited liability partnership (LLP). The structure you choose affects your liability and management responsibilities.

Research the business registration requirements in your jurisdiction, and consult with legal and financial professionals to determine the best structure for your e-commerce business.

10.2 BUSINESS LICENSES AND PERMITS

Many e-commerce businesses require licenses or permits to operate legally. The types of licenses you need depend on your location and the products or services you offer. Common examples include:

- **Business License**: This is a general license required by most businesses to operate legally. It's often issued by your local government.

- **Sales Tax Permit**: If you sell taxable products or services, you may need to obtain a sales tax permit to collect and remit sales tax to the appropriate tax authorities.

- **Specialized Permits**: Depending on your niche or location, you might require specialized permits, such as food handling permits, alcohol licenses, or health permits.

- **Home Business Permits**: If you operate your e-commerce business from your home, you may need a home business permit or zoning clearance.

- **Import/Export Licenses**: If you deal with international shipping and trade, you may need import/export licenses or permits.

Compliance with these legal requirements is crucial to avoid fines, legal issues, and disruptions to your e-commerce operations.

10.3 DATA PROTECTION AND PRIVACY

Data protection and privacy regulations are of paramount importance for e-commerce businesses, especially those that collect and process customer data. Key considerations include:

- **General Data Protection Regulation (GDPR)**: If you serve customers in the European Union (EU), you must comply with GDPR, which sets strict rules for data protection and privacy.

- **California Consumer Privacy Act (CCPA)**: If you have customers in California, you may be subject to CCPA, which grants Californian consumers certain rights regarding their personal information.

- **Data Security**: Implement robust data security measures to protect customer data from breaches and unauthorized access.

- **Privacy Policy**: Clearly communicate your data collection and processing practices through a transparent privacy policy accessible on your website.

- **Consent**: Obtain explicit consent from customers before collecting and using their personal information.

Failure to comply with data protection and privacy regulations can result in significant legal and financial consequences. Consult with legal experts to ensure your e-commerce business follows these regulations.

10.4 INTELLECTUAL PROPERTY AND TRADEMARKS

Intellectual property issues are common in e-commerce. To protect your brand and avoid legal disputes, consider the following:

- **Trademark Registration**: Register your brand's name and logo as trademarks to protect your unique identity.

- **Copyright Protection**: Ensure that the content on your website, including product descriptions, images, and blog posts, doesn't infringe on others' copyrights.

- **Counterfeits and Infringements**: Monitor your e-commerce platform for counterfeit products or violations of your intellectual property rights.

10.5 TERMS AND CONDITIONS, RETURNS, AND REFUNDS

Establish clear terms and conditions for your e-commerce store. This includes specifying your return and refund policies, payment methods, and shipping terms. Your terms and conditions should address issues such as:

- **Returns and Refunds**: Clearly define your policies for product returns, exchanges, and refunds. Be transparent about timeframes, restocking fees, and return shipping costs.

- **Payment Methods**: Detail the payment methods you accept, payment processing, and security measures to protect customer data.

- **Shipping and Delivery**: Specify shipping methods, delivery times, and costs. Make sure to communicate any potential delays or issues.

- **Dispute Resolution**: Outline the process for resolving disputes or customer complaints.

10.6 CONSUMER PROTECTION LAWS

Familiarize yourself with consumer protection laws that apply to your e-commerce business. These laws may include regulations on product safety, advertising, and pricing transparency. Compliance is vital to avoid penalties and legal issues.

10.7 CONTENT AND MARKETING COMPLIANCE

Ensure that your content, including product descriptions, advertising, and marketing materials, complies with relevant laws. Avoid false advertising, misleading claims, or deceptive practices that could result in legal consequences.

10.8 TAXES AND ACCOUNTING

Managing taxes and accounting is an essential part of e-commerce compliance. Consider the following:

- **Sales Tax**: Depending on your location and customer locations, you may need to collect and remit sales tax. Use accounting software that automates this process.

- **Income Tax**: Keep accurate financial records and work with an accountant to manage your income tax obligations.

10.9 LEGAL COUNSEL AND COMPLIANCE AUDITS

Consider seeking legal counsel to ensure your e-commerce business is compliant with all relevant laws and regulations. Periodic compliance audits can help identify and rectify potential issues before they become legal problems.

In Conclusion

Compliance with legal and regulatory requirements is crucial for the success and sustainability of your e-commerce business. Failing to address these matters can result in legal challenges, financial penalties, and damage to your brand's reputation. Stay informed about the laws and regulations that apply to your business, seek professional advice when needed, and operate with integrity to ensure your e-commerce business thrives in a legally compliant manner.

CONCLUSION

Congratulations on completing this comprehensive guide on how to run a successful e-commerce business! We've covered a wide range of topics, from the initial steps of planning and setting up your online store to the complexities of scaling and ensuring legal compliance. Here's a brief summary of the key takeaways:

1. **Starting Your E-commerce Journey**: Begin by conducting market research, selecting a niche, and choosing the right e-commerce platform for your business.

2. **Building Your E-commerce Website**: Invest in a user-friendly and visually appealing website, optimize it for search engines, and focus on mobile responsiveness.

3. **Product Selection and Sourcing**: Carefully research and select products that align with your target audience and brand, and establish strong supplier relationships.

4. **Inventory Management**: Implement efficient inventory management practices to avoid overstocking or stockouts, and consider different fulfillment methods.

5. **Brand Building**: Craft a strong and memorable brand that resonates with your audience, and utilize various marketing strategies to promote it.

6. **Marketing Your E-commerce Business**: Implement digital marketing, content marketing, and social media strategies to reach your target audience and drive sales.

7. **Customer Service and Satisfaction**: Prioritize

exceptional customer service, listen to customer feedback, and foster loyalty through loyalty programs and rewards.

8. **Scaling Your Business**: Plan and execute strategies to meet increased demand, expand your product range, and optimize operations. Pay attention to financial considerations and technology.

9. **Legal and Compliance Matters**: Ensure your e-commerce business complies with relevant laws, including business structure, licenses, data protection, intellectual property, and consumer protection.

As you move forward with your e-commerce business, remember that success often involves ongoing learning and adaptation. Keep up with industry trends, continuously improve your business operations, and stay committed to delivering exceptional products and services. Your dedication and strategic approach will pave the way for a thriving e-commerce venture.

Best of luck with your e-commerce journey, and may your online business flourish and grow! If you have any more questions or need further guidance in the future, don't hesitate to reach out.

APPENDIX: ADDITIONAL RESOURCES

In your journey to run a successful e-commerce business, you'll find that there are numerous resources available to help you navigate various aspects of the e-commerce landscape. Here are some valuable resources that can provide additional guidance, tools, and insights:

1. **E-commerce Platforms**:
   - Shopify
   - WooCommerce
   - BigCommerce
   - Magento
   - Wix

2. **Market Research Tools**:
   - Google Trends
   - SEMRush
   - Ahrefs
   - SimilarWeb
   - Statista

3. **Financial and Accounting Tools**:
   - QuickBooks
   - Xero

- Wave
- FreshBooks
- Expensify

4. **Inventory Management Software**:
   - TradeGecko
   - Stitch Labs
   - DEAR Inventory
   - inFlow Inventory
   - Zoho Inventory

5. **Email Marketing Platforms**:
   - Mailchimp
   - Constant Contact
   - SendinBlue
   - ConvertKit
   - GetResponse

6. **Legal and Compliance Resources**:
   - U.S. Small Business Administration (SBA)
   - U.S. Federal Trade Commission (FTC) - Business Center
   - European Data Protection Board (EDPB)
   - International Trademark Association (INTA)
   - World Intellectual Property Organization (WIPO)

7. **E-commerce Blogs and Forums**:
   - E-commerceFuel
   - Shopify Community
   - BigCommerce Blog
   - A Better Lemonade Stand
   - Reddit's r/ecommerce

8. **E-commerce Books**:
   - "E-commerce Evolved" by Tanner Larsson
   - "Contagious: How to Build Word of Mouth in the Digital Age" by Jonah Berger
   - "Hooked: How to Build Habit-Forming Products" by Nir Eyal
   - "The Lean Startup" by Eric Ries
   - "Influence: The Psychology of Persuasion" by Robert Cialdini

9. **E-commerce Courses and Webinars**:
   - Coursera
   - Udemy
   - LinkedIn Learning
   - HubSpot Academy
   - eCommerce Insiders

10. **Legal and Regulatory Websites**:
    - United States Copyright Office
    - United States Patent and Trademark Office (USPTO)
    - European Union General Data Protection Regulation (GDPR)
    - Federal Trade Commission (FTC) - Business Guidance
    - World Trade Organization (WTO)

11. **Industry Associations**:
    - National Retail Federation (NRF)
    - Internet Retailer
    - eCommerce Europe
    - National Association of Software and Service Companies (NASSCOM)

Remember that the e-commerce landscape is constantly evolving, so staying informed and learning from industry experts and resources is crucial for your business's success. Explore these resources, stay updated, and continue to refine your e-commerce strategies.

www.ingramcontent.com/pod-product-compliance
Lightning Source LLC
Chambersburg PA
CBHW062347290526

45794CB00005B/2130